Creative Christmas

Joan Chambers and Molly Hood

First published in 1994 by
BELAIR PUBLICATIONS LTD.
P.O. Box 12, Twickenham, TW1 2QL,
England

Series Editor Robyn Gordon
Series Designer Richard Souper
Photography by Kelvin Freeman
Typesetting by Belair
Printed and Bound through World Print Ltd

ISBN 0 947882 43 X

INTRODUCTION

This book has been written for parents and teachers to provide simple Christmas art ideas, which are adaptable for children of all ages.

Most of the materials are simple and readily available, but are supplemented by items such as coloured foil, gold and silver pens, glitter, old Christmas cards, doilies, ribbons, lace, wrapping paper, gold spray paint, etc.

For teachers in particular, historical ideas have been included, and display suggestions are incorporated in the photographs.

Many of the ideas can be used to make Christmas cards, calendars, mobiles and decorations.

**Joan Chambers
and Molly Hood**

Special thanks are due to Alexandra and Stephen Chambers for artwork and invaluable support, and to Alexandra in particular for the cover artwork.

CONTENTS

ANGEL

White crêpe paper
Small piece of white cardboard
Clear adhesive tape
Glitter, scraps of tinsel, gold foil
Felt-tip pens
Scissors and glue

1. Using cardboard, cut out a strip with a head shape as shown above.
2. Cut a rectangle of white crêpe paper. Gather it around the neck with adhesive tape to make the dress.

3. Cut a smaller rectangle of crêpe paper. Wrap a piece of adhesive tape tightly around the middle to form the sleeves. Stretch the edge of the paper to make the sleeves wider. Attach to the body with tape.
4. Decorate with glue and glitter. When dry, this stiffens the skirt and enables the figure to stand up. Add foil hair, draw a face with felt-tip pens, and add tinsel.

NATIVITY SCENE

Dark blue paper for background
Card for figures and animals
Crêpe paper in various colours
Corrugated cardboard or pieces of
  cardboard box
Yellow tissue paper
Small box covered in brown tissue (for
  manger)
Silver stars
Piece of gold or silver foil for large star
Felt-tip pens
Scissors and glue

1. Cut cardboard to make figures. (See
   angel.)
2. Cut rectangle of crêpe paper and
   decorate with felt-tip pens and glitter,
   before making the clothes. Add
   rectangles of crêpe paper for the
   head-dresses. Complete the figures as
   in angel photograph.
3. Make the baby Jesus by wrapping a
   strip of white crêpe paper round a
   small piece of card. Draw the face
   with felt-tip pens.
4. Cut strips of corrugated cardboard
   and glue together to form a stable.
   Use Plasticine or small boxes to make
   it stand upright.
5. Make the back of the stable from
   cardboard. Make animal heads and
   glue on top of this.
6. Make straw by cutting several layers
   of yellow tissue paper into narrow
   strips. (If possible, use a cutter for this.)
7. Use gold foil to make a star.

STARS

Hanging Star

Art straws
Scraps of tinsel, foil and other Christmas
   decorations
Adhesive tape, strong glue
Scissors

1. Make a star shape using straws.
   Attach them in the centre with
   adhesive tape.
2. Decorate with tinsel by rolling
   adhesive tape around and pressing
   the tinsel onto it. Press it on to the
   centre on both sides, back and front.
3. Cut slits in the end of each straw and
   place a foil shape inside, using glue to
   keep it in place.
4. Add foil and other scraps to decorate
   the star.

Fold-over Star

2 squares of foil or foil wrapping paper,
   one larger than the other
Tinsel or shiny scraps
Scissors and glue

1. Fold the larger square of paper in
   half, then in half again, forming four
   small squares. Open out and cut
   along each fold, approximately three-
   quarters of the length.
2. On each square glue the two opposite
   points together to form one section of
   the star. Repeat until four sections are
   complete.
3. Do the same with the smaller square.
   Glue the smaller star to the centre of
   the larger one. Decorate with tinsel or
   scraps.

DECORATED ROOM

Paper or card for background

Piece of wallpaper, larger than the card above

Scraps of coloured paper

Tinsel, glitter

Felt-tip pens and gold pens

Scissors and glue

1. To make the background, cover a piece of paper or card with a larger piece of wallpaper. Fold the edges over and glue down at the back.
2. Using coloured paper, make objects to go in the room, e.g. tree, window, furniture, fireplace, pictures, curtains.
3. Decorate the room with tinsel, garlands and bows.
4. Add small details, e.g. candles, Christmas cards, gifts and tree decorations.

● Make a plan for decorating a classroom, for example window, door, walls and ceiling decorations.
● Draw the front of your house and decorate it with Christmas shapes.
● Make your picture into a Christmas card or enlarge it to make a wall display.

SYMMETRICAL STAINED GLASS WINDOW

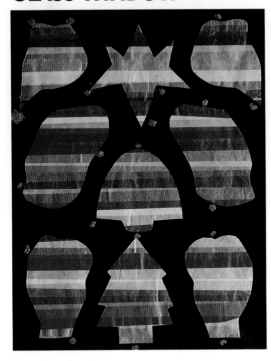

Black paper
Thin white paper for template (the same
   size as the black paper)
Strips of coloured tissue paper the same
   width as (or wider than) the white
   paper
Adhesive (or masking) tape
Large piece of tissue paper
Thin white crayon/white pencil
Sharp scissors and glue stick

1. Fold the white paper in half
   (lengthways).
2. Starting at the fold, draw half a
   Christmas shape. Repeat along the
   fold with other shapes. Cut the shapes
   out from the fold.
3. Keep the paper folded and draw
   more shapes. Push the scissors through
   the two thicknesses and cut these
   shapes out, leaving the outside edge
   intact.
4. Open the white paper out and place it

exactly on top of the black. Use a
small piece of tape on the corners to
keep it in place.
5. Draw round the inside edge with the
white crayon. Remove white template.
6. Push the points of the scissors through
the middle of each shape and cut the
shape out.
7. Glue round the edge of each shape
with a glue stick. Lay the strips of
tissue paper across the whole picture.
Overlap these.
8. Glue the large piece of tissue on to the
back and trim the surplus.

CHRISTMAS BELLS

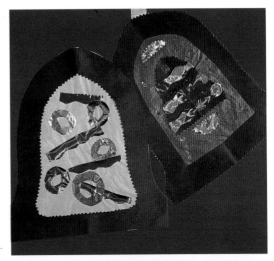

Fold a piece of black paper in half and
draw half a bell. Draw a smaller half
bell shape inside this. Keep the paper
folded and cut along both lines. Open
out and glue two layers of tissue paper
across the back. Trim and decorate with
foil, scraps, glitter, etc. Make several
shapes at the same time by holding three
or four layers of paper together and
cutting these out.

CRACKERS

Cardboard rolls

Tissue paper at least twice the length of the rolls, in various colours

Scraps of foil paper, tissue paper, tinsel, wrapping paper, etc.

Christmas cards

Pinking scissors

Scissors and glue

1. Place two or three pieces of contrasting tissue paper on top of each other and wrap around to make the cracker.

2. Twist the ends and tie with ribbon.

3. Decorate using scrap materials.

● Try these variations:
  - use pinking scissors to fringe the ends and make strips for decoration.
  - vary the length of the tissue paper.
  - cut motifs from Christmas cards and wrapping paper.
  - make miniature crackers to hang on the tree from crêpe paper, foil or wrapping paper.

WRAPPING PAPER

Sheets of white or coloured paper and
tissue paper
Polystyrene scraps
Small pieces of card
Pastry cutter in Christmas shape, e.g.
tree, star, bell
Paint and brushes
Crayons with wrappers removed
Felt-tip pens, gold pen
Pencil, scissors

Star Paper

Cut out a star shape from card. Fold it in
half and cut out a small star from the
inside. Place the large star underneath a
sheet of thin paper. Using the side of a
crayon, rub over the shape. Move the star
around underneath the paper to make an
all-over pattern. Use the smaller star in the
same way to complete the design.

● Try this technique using a holly leaf
shape.

Tissue Paper Tree

Cut a Christmas shape from a piece of
polystyrene. Draw details by pressing a
pencil into the polystyrene shape. Paint
the surface and press on to the paper.
Repeat to cover the paper. When dry,
decorate with gold pen.

Doily-patterned Paper

Try spraying gold paint through a paper
doily. Print patterns using pastry cutters
dipped in paint. Make a cardboard star
template and brush paint in an outward
direction all around the shape. Decorate
these with gold pens and felt-tip pens.

CHRISTMAS STAMPS AND ENVELOPES

Plain envelopes
White and coloured paper for the
   stamps
Narrow strips of paper for the border
Pinking scissors
Felt-tip pens

1. Decorate envelopes on the front and
   back using felt-tip pens.
2. Cut out stamps with pinking scissors or
   ordinary scissors, cut small zig-zags to
   create a serrated edge.
3. Decorate the edges and design
   pictures with felt-tip pens.
4. To make the border, fold strips of
   white paper in half and then half

again. Cut into the folded edge to
make a holly leaf. Open out the strip
and glue down.

● Design matching note-paper and
   make a set of stationery for a gift.
● Decorate a plain aerogramme with
   Christmas designs.
● Write Christmas greetings in other
   languages.
● Collect information about postal dates,
   domestic and overseas.
● Design a poster with the slogan 'Post
   Early for Christmas'.

CHRISTMAS CARDS

Coloured cardboard, e.g. green or red
White paper circle
Small pieces of green tissue paper
Felt-tip pens
Scraps of shiny paper, glitter pen
Scissors and glue

Coloured cardboard
Foil
Pieces of doily
Shiny scraps for decorations
Felt-tip pens
Scissors and glue

Holly Wreath Card
1. Fold a piece of coloured cardboard in half.
2. Draw a Christmas picture on a white paper circle and colour it.
3. Glue it on to the front of the card.
4. Spread glue around the edge of the circle and press pieces of green tissue paper on to it.
5. Decorate freely using shiny scraps and glitter.

● Try using another shape, e.g. bell, tree, star, etc. instead of a circle.

Cracker Card
1. Fold a rectangle of coloured cardboard in half.
2. Cut out two V-shapes along the top fold and along the bottom edge, to make the cracker shape.
3. Draw and cut out a smaller cracker shape from foil. Glue it on to the front of the cracker. Decorate the ends with white doily. Colour the doily.
4. Decorate the cracker using Christmas scraps.
5. Make a small cracker to go inside with the message.

CHRISTMAS CARDS

Fireplace Card

Coloured cardboard
Pieces of card
Foil scraps
Pieces of coloured paper
Gold string
Glitter
Felt-tips
Scissors and glue

1. Fold a piece of coloured card in half.
2. Start at the bottom and cut out a rectangle shape. Glue paper round the edge of the shape to make the fireplace. Glue on a piece of foil to make a mirror. Decorate the wall.
3. Keep the card closed and draw a pencil line round the inside of the fireplace.
4. Make a fire from coloured paper.
5. Glue small, decorated stockings on to a string and attach behind the fireplace with adhesive tape.

Snowy Landscape Card

Coloured cardboard in blue or turquoise
White paper
Silver and blue foil
Glitter, silver pen
Scissors and glue

1. Cut out white paper hills and glue down on to blue card.
2. Hold two or three layers of silver paper together. Draw a tree on the top layer and cut round the shape through all the layers to make several trees at once. Add details.

SNOWFLAKES

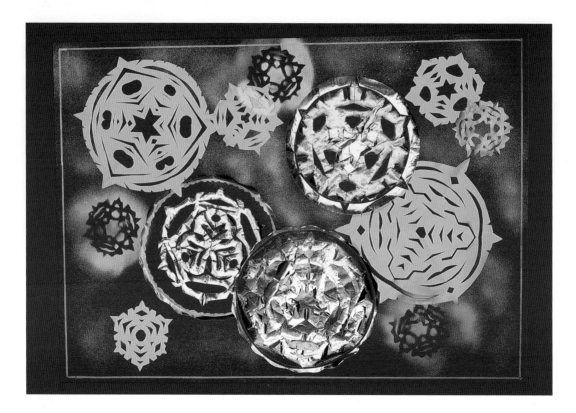

These are all based on the six-pointed snowflake.

1. Cut a circle from white paper. Fold it in half to form a semicircle. Fold the semicircle into thirds.
2. Holding this at the pointed end, cut out a sharp point at each side of the shape. This forms the six small points of the snowflake.

3. Keep it folded and cut small shapes from the folded edges. Open out and glue on to a brightly coloured background.
4. Repeat this using a variety of coloured papers. Use one as a template to spray shapes on to the background.
5. Make a multi-coloured pattern by using several different colours of foil in the spaces. Glue these back to back to make mobiles.

● These could be made in a variety of sizes and hung individually from pieces of tinsel or paper chains.
● String two or three snowflakes together, one under the other, to hang against a window.
● Use the snowflakes for the cover of a Winter book.

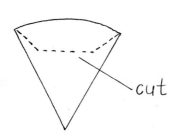

cut

SNOWMAN SCENE

Blue paper for background
Shiny blue paper
White paper
White card for stars
White crêpe paper
Scraps of coloured paper
Glitter
Can of snow spray
Felt-tip pens
Scissors and glue

1. Draw and cut out snowmen from the white paper. Spread glue on the snowman's body and press the crêpe paper loosely on to this to create a crinkled effect. Trim round the edge.
2. Make hats and scarves from coloured paper scraps and draw the details with felt-tip pens.

3. Add lake, hills and snowflakes. Make the snowflakes by gluing three short strips together. Use one of these as a template and spray over it, using snow spray. Repeat the pattern to create an interesting background.

● To make this scene into a mobile, use card instead of white paper. Hang the shapes separately in front of the blue background. Cut foil paper into zig-zag shapes to make icicles to hang above the scene. Cover a ruler with crêpe paper to suspend the scene.
● To make a background for a large display, cover first with dark blue or black paper. Use the can of spray to create hills and falling snow.

CHRISTMAS ROOFTOP

Black paper for background
Coloured paper for roof
White paper
Red and brown tissue paper
Scraps of foil and coloured paper
Cotton wool for beard
White paint or crayon for stars
Felt-tip pens, glitter
Scissors and glue

1. Using coloured paper, cut out a roof and chimney. Glue on to the background.
2. Draw a round head and body on the white paper. Cut out and spread glue over the body. Crumple red tissue paper on to the body to pad it out.
3. Spread glue around the edge of the back of the body and cover with a sheet of red tissue paper. Fold the surplus tissue paper on to the glued edge at the back.
4. Make legs, arms and hat from coloured paper. Add details using other scraps of paper, felt-tip pens and cotton wool.
5. Make a sack from the brown tissue paper and fill with toys. Glue Father Christmas and his sack on to the background.
6. Decorate the picture using crayon, glitter and scraps of paper.

THE THREE KINGS

Blue paper for background
Yellow paper for sand
Pieces of tissue paper in various colours
Green and brown paper for palm trees
Coloured paper
Scraps of shiny paper, sequins
Glitter
Gold and silver pens
Felt-tip pens
Silver and gold pens
Scissors and glue

1. Make sand hills from the yellow paper, and glue down.
2. Cut out palm trees using the green and brown paper, and glue down.
3. Cut out three identical triangles from
 * coloured paper to make bodies. Glue these down.
4. Add one arm to each figure and make faces.
5. Make tissue paper cloaks and gifts.
6. Add details in felt-tip pens.
7. Decorate with scraps of foil, sequins and glitter.

● This could be made by groups of children to form a large wall display. Draw figures and dress them to create a three dimensional display.
● Make a picture of crown designs using collage materials.

SURPRISE PLUM PUDDING

1. Draw a round shape on brown paper. Cut it out.
2. To make the flaps, fold the pudding in half and make two parallel cuts into the fold.
3. Open out and cut at one end to open the flap. Repeat several times.
4. Glue the pudding on to white paper and cut round it.
5. Make silver charms from silver foil and glue in the spaces under the flaps.
6. Place a piece of white paper under the pudding and draw round it. Cut it out and cut a wavy shape across it to make the sauce. Glue it on to the top of the pudding.
7. Glue this on to a piece of wrapping paper, then on the coloured card.
8. Turn over, spread glue along one side and press a crepe paper strip on to it to make a frill. Repeat along each side.
9. Decorate freely with felt-tip pens.

● This could make a large advent calendar.

FOIL FANS

Strips of foil in a variety of colours
Pinking scissors (optional)
Gold and silver ribbon and cord
Scissors and glue

1. Cut a variety of coloured foil paper into strips. Using a glue stick, join them together to make a large piece of paper. Leave to dry.
2. Fan fold the paper. Keep the folds together and cut diagonally across one end - use sharp scissors for this. For a lacy effect, keep the folds together and cut some V shapes into the folds.

3. Try cutting some strips of foil with pinking scissors, and glue these on to the paper before fan-folding.

● These could be made into miniature fans to hang on a Christmas tree.
● After gluing the strips together, leave to dry and use as a decorative background for Christmas artwork.
● Cut the striped paper into large Christmas shapes, or into strips for borders.

PLACE SETTING

This is a way of recycling used Christmas cards.

Hat and Napkin Ring

Cut a strip of card long enough to make a hat. Cover by wrapping a strip of red crêpe paper around the card. Wind a narrow strip of green crêpe paper on top of this. Cut some thin strips to hang down at the back. Decorate with pictures cut from Christmas cards. Repeat with small card to make the napkin ring.

Placemat

Cut a shape, e.g. stocking, bell, star. Use this as a template to make several shapes cut from Christmas cards. Glue these on to white paper and cut around, leaving a white border. Decorate the placemat with these. Find a card that has four decorative corners. Glue on to the placemat.

Place-card

Fold a small piece of red card in half. Draw a pattern with pen. Fold a smaller piece of white paper in half. Cut a wavy shape and glue down to look like snow. Cut out and decorate a chimney and glue on to the roof.

● Design a matching cracker.

CHRISTMAS CARD PATTERN

A used Christmas card with bright
  colours and a decorative border
Card or paper for background in a
  contrasting colour
Scissors and glue

1. Cut the border off and cut it into
  several pieces. Put to one side.
2. Cut the rest of the card into strips or
  shapes.
3. Carefully arrange these on the
  background paper to re-assemble the
  picture. Leave a space between each
  piece and glue down.
4. Add the pieces of border to make a
  frame.
5. Decorate with pens and glitter if
  desired.

● Use as a calendar, greetings card or
  placemat.

CHRISTMAS WREATH

Cardboard ring
Strips of green crêpe paper (cut from the
   end of a roll)
Narrow strip of foil or ribbon
Small pine cones (sprayed gold if
   preferred)
Scraps of ribbon and green foil
Scissors and glue

1. Glue one end of a strip of crêpe
   paper on to the ring. Wrap this round
the ring, overlapping it, and glue the
end down.
2. Fringe along one side of another
   folded crêpe paper strip. Open out
   and wrap around the ring as in
   step 1.
3. Decorate with trimmings.
4. To make into a picture, glue on to a
   door made from coloured card. Add
   details using shiny paper and felt-tip
   pens.

TREE DECORATIONS

Card cut into circles, rings, bells, trees
Scraps of foil in various colours
Strips of foil in medium and narrow widths
Gold pen and glitter
Pinking scissors (optional)
Scissors and glue

1. Cover some circles with foil. Fold strips in half and half again, and cut small shapes out of the folded edges. Open out and use to decorate the circle back and front. Cover other circles with strips of foil, some cut with pinking scissors.
2. Cover rings by winding medium strips of foil around the shapes. Repeat with narrow strips in a contrasting colour. Decorate with holly or curled strips.
3. Cover bells with foil. Use scraps of shiny materials to decorate both sides.
4. Make three identical tree shapes. Fold them in half and glue each half back to back to form a three dimensional shape.
5. Decorate with foil and pens.

● Cut large rings of cardboard, cover in foil and hang small decorations inside. Add thin strips of foil to complete the mobile.
● Make large versions of the tree decorations to suspend from the ceiling, and use in Christmas displays.
● Use the decorations to make Christmas cards or to complete Christmas party hats.

THE TWELVE DAYS OF CHRISTMAS

1. Using cream paper, cut out twelve rectangles.
2. Cut wavy patterns along each side and edge with gold pen.
3. Decorate each scroll with a picture to represent each of the twelve days of Christmas and write the number of the day.
4. Glue on to a wrapping paper background keeping the top and bottom edges rolled.
5. Decorate with ribbons and pens.

On the first day of Christmas,
My true love sent to me
A partridge in a pear tree.

On the second day of Christmas,
My true love sent to me
Two turtles doves,
And a partridge in a pear tree.
   etc.
Third - three French hens
Fourth - four colly birds
Fifth - five gold rings
Sixth - six geese a-laying
Seventh - seven swans a-swimming
Eighth - eight maids a-milking
Ninth - nine ladies dancing
Tenth - ten lords a-leaping
Eleventh - eleven pipers piping
Twelfth - twelve drummers drumming

VICTORIAN CHRISTMAS TREE

Card or paper for tree and background
Green crêpe paper strips
White paper for decorations
Felt-tip pens, gold pen
Coloured paper scraps
Scissors and glue

1. Draw a Christmas tree on the card or paper. Cut it out and spread glue over the lower part.

2. Starting at the bottom of the tree, push the crêpe paper on to the glue to create a frilled effect. Repeat with each frill overlapping slightly.
3. Turn the tree over and trim.
4. Glue on to a background and make a decorative pot from coloured paper.
5. Draw decorations using felt-tip pens. Cut these out and glue on to the tree, e.g. flags, candles, candy canes, toys, cones, drums.

VICTORIAN CARDS

Some Victorian cards were flat like a postcard and cut into unusual shapes.

Cut pastel coloured card, e.g. cream or pale green, into the shapes shown above. These include a cross, crescent, tambourine, drum and artist's palette. Draw round the edge with gold pen and draw pictures with coloured pencils. Popular themes in Victorian cards included:

flowers: holly, ivy, pansies, violets, irises, fuchsias, forget-me-nots,
animals in clothing of the period, e.g. frogs, cats, dogs, bats, insects,
food - turkeys, plum puddings.

The rectangular card in the bottom centre of the photograph above is a reproduction of the first Christmas card. It was designed by John Calcott-Horsley in 1843. There were one thousand copies made and each one was coloured by hand.

- Here are some typical messages found on Victorian Christmas cards:
  'A Christmas greeting now I send, To you my dear and loving friend.'
  'Very happy may it be, Christmas time to thine and thee.'
- Design pop-up versions of Victorian cards.

VICTORIAN FAN CARD

6 rectangles of card in a pastel colour
Reproduction Christmas scraps or
  pictures from used Christmas cards
Christmas gift wrapping paper, dark
  green or dark red
One butterfly pin
Gold pen
Scissors and glue

1. Draw one section of the fan on a
   rectangle of card. (See photograph for
   shape.)
2. Cut it out and use as a template to
   make five other sections.
3. Decorate the end of each section with
   wrapping paper and Christmas

pictures. Draw around the edge of
each shape with gold pen.
4. Make a hole through the middle of
   each one at the lower end with a
   sharp pair of scissors. Holding them
   all together, push the butterfly pin
   through so that the sections will
   fan out.
5. Write the words 'Merry Christmas and
   a Happy New Year' across the fan.

● Close the fan and make an envelope
  to fit. Decorate with Victorian flowers,
  e.g. pansies, violets and ivy.
● Make a modern version using bright
  colours, e.g. red, yellow, green.

TUDOR CUSHION

Pink or white card

Piece of white or cream net or old stocking

Lace edging - or paper doily

Pot-pourri

Silver or gold foil

Ribbon

Adhesive tape

Small artificial flowers (or make flowers from tissue paper)

Scissors and glue

1. Cut a circle from the card and spread glue all over it. Press the pot-pourri into the glue and leave to dry.

2. Cover with the net or stocking and tape on to the back.

3. Decorate with strips of foil. Attach the ends at the back.

4. Pleat the lace around the edge at the back. Use adhesive tape or strong glue.

5. Decorate with flowers and a ribbon loop for hanging.

● This could be made into a gift by attaching it to a piece of card.

TUDOR GIFT BOX

A small cardboard box with a lid
Silver or gold tissue paper or white tissue
    paper sprayed with gold paint
Gold and silver foil
Gold and silver pens
Clear adhesive tape
Scissors and glue

1. Cover the box with tissue paper and
    decorate it with scraps of foil and
    metallic pens.
2. To make a rose, fold a strip of tissue
    paper in half lengthways.
3. Keep the folded edge at the top and
gather the lower edges together.
4. Secure the flowers using adhesive
    tape. Glue on to the lid.

● Make sweetmeats from marzipan,
    nuts, dried fruit and mixed peel.
    Design your own shapes, e.g. circle,
    plaited shapes, diamond, twists.
● The box can be used for other gifts.
● Use silver foil and cardboard to make
    a mirror. Decorate it with Tudor roses
    and gold and silver leaves. Use this
    technique for making flowers to
    decorate other historical objects.

MEDIEVAL CANDLESTICK

Yellow paper or card for background
Gold doily (spray a white doily with
   gold paint)
Green, white and blue paper
Gold and blue pen
Scissors and glue

1. Fold a rectangle of blue paper in half
   lengthways and draw half a
   candlestick, starting at the fold. Cut
   out the shape and open out.
2. Place the blue candlestick on the gold
   doily and draw around it. Cut this
   shape out of the doily and glue down.
   Decorate using strips of blue paper.

3. Make a candle from white paper and
   decorate it. Glue it down.
4. Draw an archway with a pencil. Draw
   two straight lines for the pillars. Cut a
   semi-circle of card the width of the
   pillars and draw around the curved
   part to create the arch. Decorate with
   blue and gold felt-tip pens.
5. Put two or three layers of green paper
   on top of each other and cut out leaf
   shapes. Fringe the edges. Glue at the
   base of the candlestick.

● This could be used as a greetings card
   or calendar.

MEDIEVAL MUSIC BOOK AND BOOKMARK

Two pieces of card the same size
Blue tissue paper - larger than the card
Rectangle of thin card for the spine
Cotton wool cut from a roll
Gold foil
White or cream paper
Felt-tip pens, gold pen
Scraps of paper
Scissors and glue

1. Gently stretch the cotton wool to fit the front cover. Glue it down.
2. Spread glue around the edges of the back. Press the tissue paper over the cover on to the glue. Repeat with another layer of blue tissue paper.

Glue a piece of paper on the inside of the cover to neaten the edges.
3. Make the back cover the same way, without using the cotton wool.
4. Write out the words of some Medieval Christmas carols (for example, 'Coventry Carol' and 'Noel, Noel') on cream paper and decorate the border.
5. Cover the spine with gold foil. Glue it on to the two covers.
6. Decorate carefully with gold pen, illuminated letters and Medieval pictures.

● Using gold card, make a decorative bookmark to match the music book.

For details of further Belair Publications,
please write to:
BELAIR PUBLICATIONS LTD.,
P.O. Box 12, Twickenham, TW1 2QL,
England.

For sales and distribution (outside USA
and Canada):
FOLENS PUBLISHERS, Albert House,
Apex Business Centre, Boscombe Road,
Dunstable, Beds., LU5 4RL, England.